·Portfoolio 20·

THE YEAR'S BEST CANADIAN EDITORIAL CARTOONS

EDITED WITH TEXT BY **GUY BADEAUX**

McArthur
&
Company

Published in Canada in 2004 by
McArthur & Company
322 King St. West, Suite 402
Toronto, Ontario M5V 1J2
www.mcarthur-co.com

Library and Archives Canada has catalogued this publication as follows:
          Portfoolio : the year in Canadian caricature
Annual.
Subtitle varies.
Imprint varies.
Includes some text in French.
ISSN 0839-6485
ISBN 1-55278-446-0 (volume 20)

          1. Canada—Politics and government—1984-   -Caricatures and cartoons.
2. World politics—Caricatures and cartoons. 3. Canadian wit and humor, Pictorial.
I. Title: Portfolio.

NC1300.P67   971.064'7'0267   C89-030416-5 rev

The publisher would like to acknowledge the financial support of the Government of
Canada through the Book Publishing Industry Development Program, the Canada Council
for the Arts, and the Ontario Arts Council for our publishing activities. We also acknowledge
the Government of Ontario through the Ontario Media Development Corporation Ontario
Book Initiative.

Edited by: **Guy Badeaux**
Text by: **Guy Badeaux**
Guy Badeaux is editorial cartoonist for *Le Droit* in Ottawa.

Design by: **Mathilde Hébert**
Printed in Canada by Transcontinental Printers

Bush finally discovers a weapon of mass destruction

SERGE CHAPLEAU, *La Presse*, Montreal, June 7, 2003

Going home?

CÔTÉ, *Le Soleil,* Quebec, February 12, 2003

CORRIGAN, *The Toronto Star*, November 7, 2003

Photograph

Where the war of words gives way to images.

It's now obvious to most that Saddam Hussein probably never had weapons of mass destruction in his arsenal. As the US and Britain sink into the quagmire that is now Iraq, "sexed-up" dossiers and futile attempts to link Saddam to Al-Qaida also mar their credibility.

Bolstered for a time by the capture of the man himself, American fortunes would soon sink to a new low when photos of caskets draped in the American flag appeared in print soon to be followed by others showing American soldiers degrading Iraqi prisoners in Abu Ghraib prison. Failing to take advantage of this public relations bonanza, terrorist groups in Iraq kidnap American, as well as coalition forces support personnel, and broadcast their beheadings on the web.

Meanwhile, back in the US, the commission of inquiry on the events leading up to September 11 tables its report. While not blaming anyone in particular, the CIA director is compelled to tender his resignation.

PASCAL, *The Gazette*, Montreal

OLSON, *The Vancouver Courier*

CLEMENT, *The National Post*

CORRIGAN, *The Toronto Star*

CLEMENT, *The National Post*

AISLIN, *The Gazette*, Montreal

CUMMINGS, *The Winnipeg Free Press*

SHAHIB

QUEER EYE FOR THE VERY BAD GUY

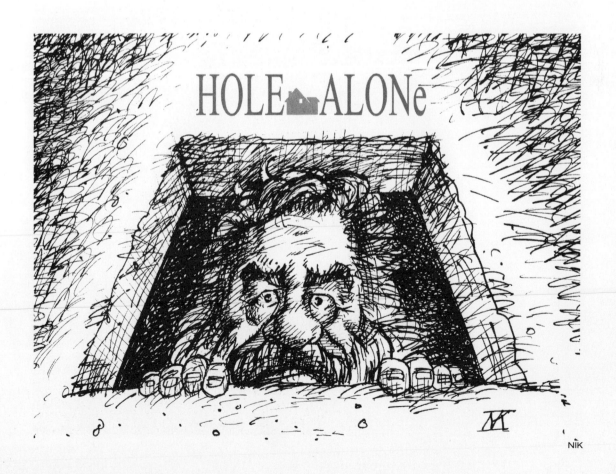

MACKAY, *The Hamilton Spectator*

GABLE, *The Globe & Mail*

ANDY, *The National Post*

PETERSON, *The Vancouver Sun*

We will vanquish terrorism!

DEA, *La Presse*, Montreal

TAB, *The Calgary Sun*

KRIEGER, *The Province*, Vancouver

AISLIN, *The Gazette*, Montreal

LIND, *Weltschmerz*

BADO, *Le Droit*, Ottawa

PETERSON, *The Vancouver Sun*

CLEMENT, *The National Post*

GABLE, *The Globe & Mail*

CUMMINGS, *The Winnipeg Free Press*

McCULLOUGH

MACKINNON, *The Chronicle-Herald*, Halifax

CLEMENT, *The National Post*

.23

THE WALL—

A. SHARON

It's A Man's Man's World

Where wars and terrorist attacks take centre stage and xenophobia casts Sonia Gandhi aside.

While construction may be booming in Israel, the "roadmap to peace" is still but a blueprint. Ariel Sharon, despite his stated intention to withdraw from the Gaza Strip, is rebuffed by his own Likoud party. The protective wall, notwithstanding a non-binding condemnation by the International Court in The Hague, continues to inch its way through the West Bank while targeted assassinations continue apace.

Meanwhile in Haiti, opposition rebels occupy half the country, forcing President Jean-Bertrand Aristide into exile. Flown by American forces to Central Africa, he accuses them of kidnapping as soon as he gets off the plane. The immediate response is that he was on the brink of being accused of drug trafficking and arrested anyway. After a brief sojourn in the Caribbean's, he finally finds refuge in South Africa. By an ironic turn of events, both the US and French armies send troops to Haiti in order to keep the peace. A small Canadian contingent is also sent there but, if we can manage to say this with a straight face, the bulk of our forces is stationed in Afghanistan.

Two reversals of fortune also mark the year. Libya is welcomed back in the concert of nations after Mohamar Gadhafi allows inspectors to verify that the country is not building an atomic bomb. For his part, Jose Maria Aznar is defeated in a general election after bombs explode in Madrid killing 191 people. Despite evidence pointing towards Islamic extremists, Spanish authorities are quick to blame the attack on Basque separatists. The voters, seeing this as a blatant attempt at electioneering, respond by throwing their lot with the Socialists who, as promised, pull Spanish troops from Iraq upon being sworn in.

While we're on the subject of elections, Vladimir Putin was easily re-elected in Russia. Why he would need to strengthen his hand by closing opposition TV stations and imprisoning political opponents baffles most observers. Our guess is that while you can take the colonel out of the KGB, you cannot take the KGB out of he colonel.

Road Map

CÔTÉ, *Le Soleil*, Quebec

TAB, *The Calgary Sun*

26.

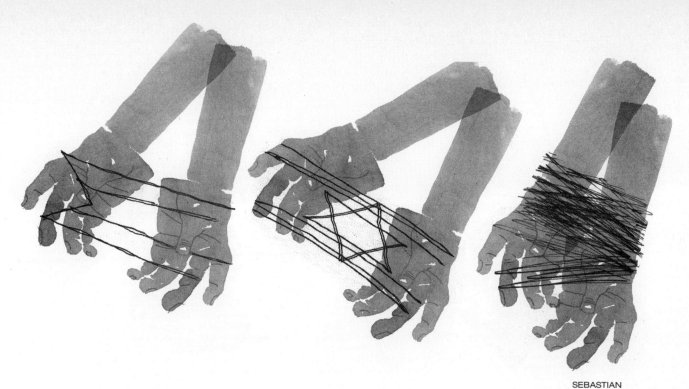

SEBASTIAN

GARNOTTE, *Le Devoir*, Montreal

– I'm leaving in order to avoid a bloodbath!

GARNOTTE, *Le Devoir*, Montreal

McCULLOUGH

TAB, *The Calgary Sun*

PASCAL, *The Gazette*, Montreal

RODEWALT, *The Calgary Herald*

CUMMINGS, *The Winnipeg Free Press*

AISLIN, *The Gazette*, Montreal

PASCAL, *The Gazette*, Montreal

JENKINS, *The Globe & Mail*

CUMMINGS, *The Winnipeg Free Press*

RODEWALT, unpublished

CUMMINGS, *The Winnipeg Free Press*

GABLE, *The Globe & Mail*

BADO, *Le Droit*, Ottawa

Everybody Is a Star

Where stars strip and politicians drape themselves in the Stars and Stripes.

The Jackson family was back in the news again this year although some members, thanks to "wardrobe malfunction", were more visible than others. But enough about music.

Hollywood was not to be outdone. Arnold Schwarzenegger became Governor of California last summer, Michael Moore won the Palme d'Or at the Cannes film festival for his anti George W. Bush *Fahrenheit 9/11* and Mel Gibson gave us three hours of flagellation with *The Passion Of The Christ*.

America lost, if not a great actor, one of it's most famous citizen, when Ronald Reagan passed away after a long battle with Alzheimer's disease.

Speaking of stars, Martha Stewart's trial came to a conclusion and Dubya vowed to send a manned mission to Mars.

2004 being an election year in the US, we witnessed a spirited, if lacklustre, Democratic primaries season. After an early lead fuelled by an intensive web campaign, Howard Dean blew it when he let out his famous primal scream after his defeat in Iowa. Since terrorism and patriotism were sure to become the Republican's favourite themes, Democratic voters decided to pick a candidate who would not be vulnerable on those fronts and chose John Kerry, a Vietnam war hero.

Bill Clinton published his autobiography in the summer but any fears he would steal the spotlight were put to rest when he delivered a rousing speech in support of Kerry during the Democratic Convention in Boston.

It is not clear, as we go to press, if Ralph Nader would be the spoiler yet again and allow Bush a second term.

PERRY

CAM, *The Ottawa Citizen*

MACKINNON, *The Chronicle-Herald*, Halifax

RICE

BADO, *Le Droit*, Ottawa

CLEMENT, *The National Post*

MOU, *The Toronto Star*

MACKAY, *The Hamilton Spectator*

RODEWALT, *The Calgary Herald*

HARROP, *Back Bench*

DE ADDER, *The Halifax Daily News*

BADO, *Le Droit*, Ottawa

DUSAN, *The Toronto Star*

TAB, *The Calgary Sun*

ROSEN

MURPHY, *The Province*, Vancouver

ROSEN

BADO, *Le Droit*, Ottawa

LIND, *Weltschmerz*

CLEMENT, *The National Post*

BADO, *Le Droit*, Ottawa

BADO, *Le Droit*, Ottawa

McCULLOUGH

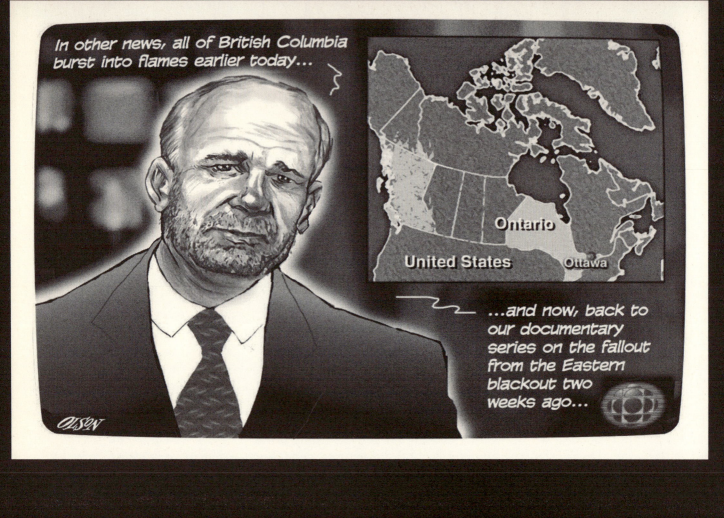

Help

Where blackouts, forest fires, mad cow disease and Dalton McGuinty plague the nation.

A blackout last August plunged Ontario as well as New England in turmoil. What was first suspected as a terrorist attack turned out to be trees obstructing power lines in Ohio.

Ontario went to the polls and, despite attack ads and a leaked memo describing Dalton McGuinty as a "pointy headed kitten-eating Martian", Ernie Eve's Conservatives were soundly defeated.

With the US ban on Canadian beef still in full force, Alberta's Ralph Klein took matters in his own hands and bypassed Ottawa by appealing directly to Washington congressmen.

Further west, forest fires were raging in British Columbia last summer, destroying 239 homes near Kelowna in its wake and forcing 30 000 people to flee. Vacationing in Hawaii, Premier Gordon Campbell had his winter holidays spoiled yet again when the RCMP raided the offices of two Liberal staffers in the B.C. legislature. Again in B.C., Svend Robinson resigned his post as Member of Parliament and pleaded guilty to the theft of a $60 000 diamond ring. He was let off with a sentence of community work and averted a criminal record which would surely have prevented him from later going to Europe on a parliamentary junket dealing with ethics in politics.

In a similar scenario, Air Canada enjoyed a reprieve and was bailed out by its creditors at the last minute. Haven't we seen this movie before?

LEFCOURT

HARROP, *Back Bench*

CAM, *The Ottawa Citizen*

CORRIGAN, *The Toronto Star*

RODEWALT, *Maclean's*

PHILLIPS, *The Toronto Sun*

54.

CAM, *The Ottawa Citizen*

ANDY, *The National Post*

AISLIN, *The Gazette*, Montreal

A World Epidemic?   CÔTÉ, *Le Soleil*, Quebec

MAYES, *The Edmonton Journal*

BRITISH COLUMBIA 2003

PETERSON, *The Vancouver Sun*

OLSON, *Maclean's*

HARROP, *The Vancouver Sun*

HARROP, *The Vancouver Sun*

OLYMPIC LOGO DESIGN COMPETITION ENTRY

RICE

OLSON, *The Vancouver Courier*

CLEMENT, *The National Post*

HARROP, *Back Bench*

MP NO MORE,
BUT ALWAYS
A POSTER BOY.

MACKAY, unpublished

Air Canada

MOU, *The Toronto Star*

DEWAR, *The Ottawa Sun*

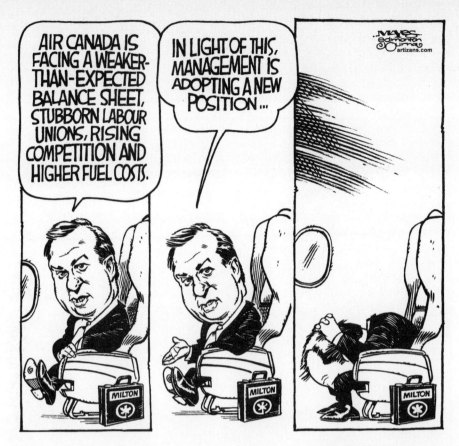

MAYES, *The Edmonton Journal*

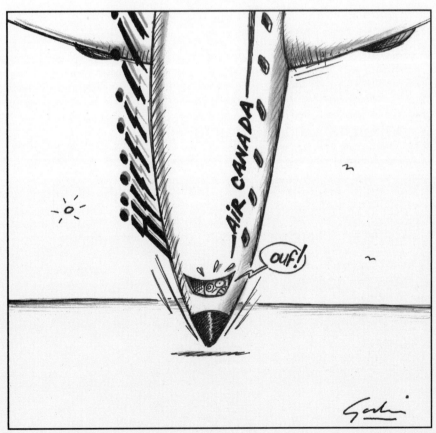

GODIN, *La Presse*, Montreal

When the Gods Gather to Gossip

Nights In White Satin

Where Canadians learn a new word as its' cultural elite wines and dines in foreign climes.

A few eyebrows were raised when it was announced that Adrienne Clarkson, our Governor General, would be taking a Circumpolar Tour of Scandinavian countries, as well as Russia, with 60 members of our cultural elite and a retinue of staffers, all for the bargain price of a million dollars. The problem was further compounded when, summoned by the House of Common's public accounts committee to explain the expense, two employees flew 1st class to Ottawa and returned promptly on the tour after testifying for a few hours. Why no one from Rideau Hall was available at the time was not fully explained. When it was later revealed that the whole shindig had cost 5 times the original estimate, our GG was safely back in Europe, alongside Elisabeth II, commemorating the 60th anniversary of D-day.

While we're on the subject of profligate Canadians, let's not forget our own Conrad Black, aka Lord Black of Crossharbour, who had to suffer the indignity of having his extravagant lifestyle questioned by Hollinger's shareholders. When the company shelled out millions to purchase the letters of Franklin Roosevelt just as Conrad was writing FDR's biography, blurring the line between his private and business expenses, they demanded nothing less than a New Deal.

On a more colourful note, Don Cherry opined on "Coach's Corner" that only European hockey players, as well as "French guys", wore visors with their helmets. This, of course, sparked outrage in some quarters and prompted the Bloc to call for his head. The CBC countered by considering a 7 seconds time delay so they could vet the rants of their biggest money-maker.

In other hockey news, Vancouver prosecutors charged the Canucks' Todd Bertuzzi with assault causing bodily harm for a sucker punch on Colorado Rockies' player Steve Moore that sent him to hospital with a fractured neck.

Of course, none of this would have happened if they had been members of the Edmonton Eskimos and on tour with Adrienne.

CORRIGAN, *The Toronto Star*

PERRY

MACKAY, *The Hamilton Spectator*

HARROP, *Back Bench*

MAYES, *The Edmonton Journal*

CUMMINGS, *The Winnipeg Free Press*

DOLIGHAN

GRASTON, *The Windsor Star*

DUSAN, *The Toronto Star*

GARNOTTE, *Le Devoir*, Montreal

MANDATORY...

AISLIN, *The Gazette*, Montreal

COACH'S CORNER

MAYES, *The Edmonton Journal*

MAYES, *The Edmonton Journal*

NEASE, *The Oakville Beaver*

MAYES, *The Edmonton Journal*

Will It Go Round In Circles

Where the Canadian government gets the run-around from the Iranian justice system just as it balks at allowing gay couples to wear a ring.

Zahra Kazemi, a Canadian freelance journalist of Iranian origin, died July 10, 2003, while in detention for taking photographs outside a Tehran prison during student-led protests against the ruling theocracy. Iranian authorities initially claimed she was victim of a stroke, but a presidential committee later found she had died of a fractured skull and brain haemorrhage. She was buried in Iran against the wishes of her son in Canada and an autopsy report was never disclosed. After international pressure, a low-level security officer was put on trial for "semi-intentional murder". He was later acquitted as the court came to the novel conclusion that Ms. Kazemi had died from a fall.

Two other Canadians citizens also had run-ins with foreign justice. William Sampson was released from prison after spending two and a half years in a Saudi jail where he faced public beheading after being convicted of carrying out bombings that killed a British man and injured several others. For his part, Maher Arar, after returning from a trip to North Africa, was arrested while in transit in New York, and, despite holding a Canadian passport, deported to Syria, where he was interrogated and detained. After a relentless campaign by his wife, he has returned to Canada where he is seeking justice. An inquiry is being held in Ottawa where most of the evidence presented is kept secret because of national security concerns. A leak to *Ottawa Citizen* journalist Juliette O'Neil prompts the RCMP to raid her house.

The year also saw the return to Canada of some members of the Khadr family, whose patriarch, killed in a shootout with American troops in Afghanistan, was suspected of being a bin Laden associate. Meanwhile, the wheels of justice are spinning as the Supreme Court ponders whether same-sex marriage is constitutional.

**FREE
TO CATCH
THE TRUTH**

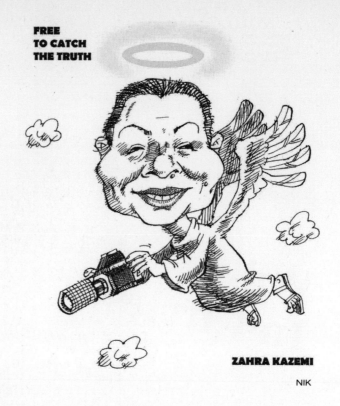

ZAHRA KAZEMI

NIK

BADO, *Le Droit*, Ottawa

Canada Responds

PETERSON, *The Vancouver Sun*

CUMMINGS, *The Winnipeg Free Press*

GABLE, *The Globe & Mail*

DUSAN, *The Toronto Star*

MACKAY, *The Hamilton Spectator*

McCULLOUGH

AL-QAIDA MOTHER

RICE

NEASE, *The Oakville Beaver*

GRASTON, unpublished

MURPHY, *The Province*, Vancouver

RICE

TAB, *The Calgary Sun*

Till Death Do Us Part

Where we learn that the united Right sticks to the tried and true and is not lured by the prospect of free auto parts.

The Alliance and the Progressive Conservative parties vote, despite their aversion to same-sex marriages, to unite their destinies and drop the "progressive" label from their name in order to better reflect the rightward shift in their policies.

After looking at the polls showing that, despite the operation, their numbers had not climbed, Peter Mackay and Bernard Lord decline to seek the leadership of the new party, leaving the field open to three contenders. Magna auto parts heiress Belinda Stronach, Alliance leader Stephen Harper and defeated Ontario cabinet minister Tom Long throw their hats in the ring. Unmoved by Belinda's "baking a bigger economic pie" cant and uninspired by Long, the Conservatives rally behind stolid Stephen Harper.

CUMMINGS, *The Winnipeg Free Press*

RODEWALT, *The Calgary Herald*

GABLE, *The Globe & Mail*

GABLE, *The Globe & Mail*

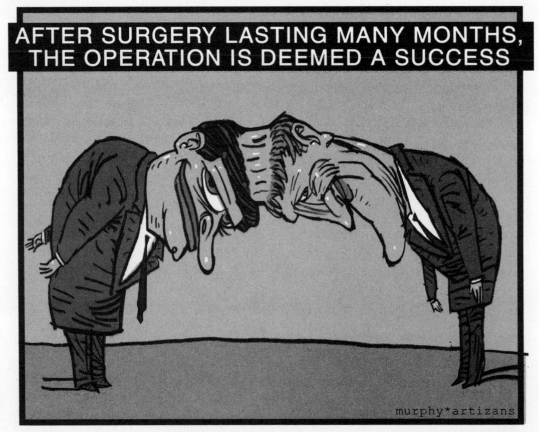

MURPHY

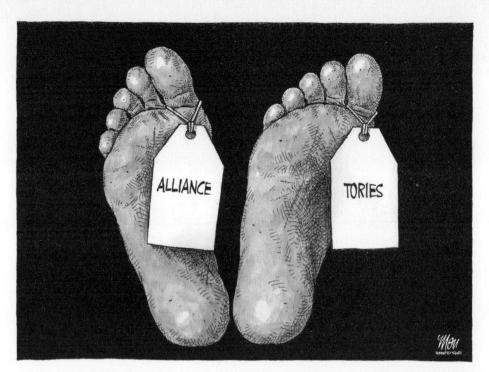

MOU, *The Toronto Star*

TAB, *The Calgary Sun*

MEET THE (COUGH) PRESS...

CAM, *The Ottawa Citizen*

ANDY, *The National Post*

NEASE, *The Oakville Beaver*

LAMONTAGNE, *Maclean's*

"AN EXCITING YOUNG BLOND WOMAN WITH LITTLE OR NO POLITICAL EXPERIENCE?....THIS BELINDA STRONACH RESUME SOUNDS VAGUELY FAMILIAR."

MAYES, *The Edmonton Journal*

PASCAL, *The Gazette*, Montreal

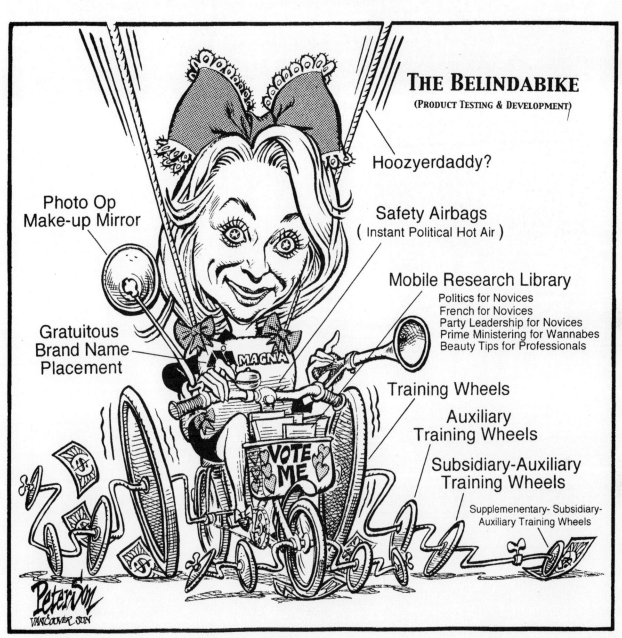

PETERSON, *The Vancouver Sun*

NEASE, *The Oakville Beaver*

MURPHY, *The Province*, Vancouver

DE ADDER, *The Halifax Daily News*

KRIEGER, *The Province*, Vancouver

It's My party

Where the old guy is replaced by… a not quite as old guy.

Paul Martin, after 9 years of waiting in the wings, finally becomes leader of the Liberal party. Bowing to pressure from within the party, Jean Chrétien steps down as Prime Minister two months ahead of schedule.

With Paul Martin at the helm, attention now shifts to possible conflicts of interest arising from his past ownership of Canada Steamship Lines. Despite having transferred control of CSL to his three adult sons in March 2003, critics argue that even if the Prime Minister stepped away from the Cabinet table when shipbuilding and marine transportation were discussed, he would still be in conflict on issues ranging from taxation of offshore companies to the Kyoto Accord, as CSL is a major shipper of coal for power-generation plants in Ontario.

Aren't we glad Howard Wilson is no longer ethics counsellor.

"striking resemblance...how many sittings did it take?"

SEBASTIAN

SNUBS BY THE U.S. AND NOW ITALY, JEAN WAS NOTICING A SUBTLE TREND...

CAM, *The Ottawa Citizen*

Chretien's greatest legacy

MURPHY, *The Province*, Vancouver

DE ADDER, *The Halifax Daily News*

GABLE, *The Globe & Mail*

RODEWALT, unpublished

POP!

NEASE, *The Oakville Beaver*

RODEWALT, *The Calgary Herald*

HARROP, *The Vancouver Sun*

TAB, *The Calgary Sun*

Hanky Panky

*Where the Liberals whitewash
their dirty laundry in public hearings.*

George Radwanski, after putting up a spirited defence to accusations of falsifying his expense account, is relieved of his post as Privacy Commissioner.

Allan Rock, for his part, puts an end to his leadership aspirations after it is revealed that he and numerous Liberal cabinet ministers had enjoyed airplane rides and fishing trips in New-Brunswick on the Irving family's tab.

Sheila Fraser tables her much anticipated final report on the sponsorship scandal, shedding light on the questionable practices of top management at Public Works, Canada Post, the Royal Mint as well as VIA Rail.

Paul Martin promises to get to the bottom of the whole thing and creates the Gomery Commission. The House of Commons also holds its' own panel of inquiry and summons Alfonso Gagliano, André Ouellet, David Dingwall, Jean Pelletier as well as Chuck Guité to testify before it. Not much was learned from their testimony, as they had kept no records and all claimed to have only followed normal business practices.

The whole thing becomes a three-ring circus as the hearings, chaired by a Conservative MP, becomes a showcase for politicians vying for attention and trying to score political points. Having volunteered to testify, Myriam Bédard, the former biathlon Olympic medallist, who had been disparaged by Pelletier as a "poor single mother", levels some wild accusations of her own. Claiming that her current boyfriend was instrumental in Canada's decision not to follow the US in the invasion of Iraq, she also alleged that Jacques Villeneuve had received millions for displaying the Canadian flag on his racing suit and that advertising company Groupaction was involved in drug trafficking.

She'd fit right in CHOI radio station in Quebec City.

CUMMINGS, *The Winnipeg Free Press*

CLEMENT, *The National Post*

PETERSON, *The Vancouver Sun*

CLEMENT, *The National Post*

HARROP, *Back Bench*

AISLIN, *The Gazette*, Montreal

CUMMINGS, *The Winnipeg Free Press*

MURPHY, *The Province*, Vancouver

CAM, *The Ottawa Citizen*

PERRY, unpublished

Alfonso is guilty! The dog and I had no idea what he was doing up there!

GARNOTTE, *Le Devoir*, Montreal

ANDY, *The National Post*

CAM, *The Ottawa Citizen*

CUMMINGS, *The Winnipeg Free Press*

JENKINS, *The Globe & Mail*

PASCAL, *The Gazette*, Montreal

MACKAY, *The Hamilton Spectator*

HARROP, *Back Bench*

Whole Lotta Shakin' Goin' On

Where Cabinet Ministers are thrown overboard by the new captain.

Paul Martin surprises most observers by excluding the other leadership contenders from his first cabinet. To distance himself further from Jean Chrétien, he decrees that, from now on, he would play no favourites and all seats would be open to challengers. Sheila Copp is especially vulnerable in Hamilton East which, because of redistribution, is also coveted by Tony Valeri, the new Transport Minister.

Meanwhile, Paul Martin goes about the normal business of a World Leader: meeting his peers, hobnobbing with religious leaders or Rock stars, and leaving to an underling the tedious business of coming up with a budget,

CORRIGAN, *The Toronto Star*

NEASE, *The Oakville Beaver*

The Comeback Kid

PETERSON, *The Vancouver Sun*

HARROP, *Back Bench*

Canada-US relations: harmony returns!
– They're swapping Jean Chretien jokes!

GARNOTTE, *Le Devoir*, Montreal

RODEWALT, *The Calgary Herald*

PETERSON, *The Vancouver Sun*

DOLIGHAN

NEASE, *The Oakville Beaver*

I want to win back my country!

DEA, *La Presse*, Montreal

AISLIN, *The Gazette*, Montreal

The state of Canadian finances...   CÔTÉ, *Le Soleil*, Quebec

GRASTON, *The Windsor Star*

Stayin' Alive

Where the Liberals barely hang on to power.

With an election in the air, the Liberals soon revert to form and, turning their back on their brand new policy of opening up the nominations, recruit a slew of star candidates. They convince Scott Brisson, an openly gay MP from Nova Scotia, Ujjal Dosanjh, an ex NDP Prime Minister of British Columbia, Jean Lapierre, a talk-show host in Montreal and founding member of the Bloc Quebecois, Glen Murray, the mayor of Winnipeg and also Ken Dryden to run unopposed in their selected ridings.

Capitalising on the weakness of the opposition and the inexperience of the Conservative's new leader, the government drop the writ. Unhappy with the Alliance domination of the Conservative Party, Joe Clark weighs in with a tepid support of Paul Martin.

The Liberals campaign on health care, day care, the cities but mostly on demonising Stephen Harper, while the Conservatives capitalise on the wasted millions in the gun registry and the sponsorship programs. Jack Layton accuses Paul Martin of being personally responsible for the death of the homeless in Toronto, while the Bloc Quebecois is left to campaign alone in Quebec where it is already 20 points ahead of the Liberals.

The Conservatives run into trouble when their official languages critic questions the scope of the Official Languages Act, MP Cheryl Gallant compares abortion to the recent beheading of an American working in Iraq and Stephen Harper himself threatens to use the notwithstanding clause to outlaw same-sex marriage if the Supreme Court ever allowed it.

Hampered in the early going of the campaign by the recent Ontario budget, the Liberal's fortunes improve when Canadian voters are frightened by the likelihood of a Conservative/Bloc coalition government.

ANDY, *The National Post*

MURPHY, *The Province*, Vancouver

STARTING BLOCKS

MACKINNON, *The Chronicle-Herald*, Halifax

MACKAY, *The Hamilton Spectator*

PERRY, *Maclean's*

LAYTON AND THE MASSES

MAKE THE RICH PAY!

GET FREE STUFF

CUMMINGS, *The Winnipeg Free Press*

MACKINNON, *The Chronicle-Herald*, Halifax

RODEWALT, *The Calgary Herald*

ANDY, *The National Post*

ALLIANCE PC ET BLOC...

CÔTÉ, *Le Soleil*, Quebec

MACKINNON, *The Chronicle-Herald*, Halifax

GRASTON, *The Windsor Star*

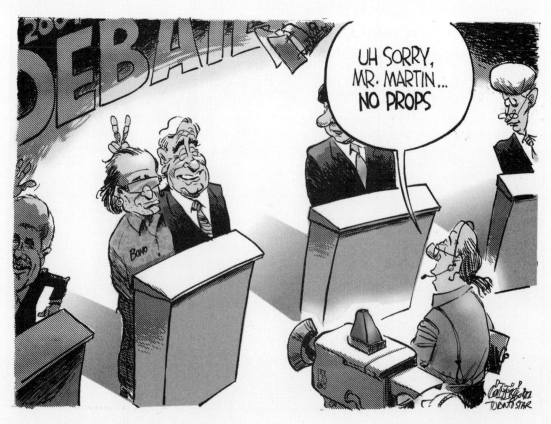

CORRIGAN, *The Toronto Star*

TAB, *The Calgary Sun*

MACKINNON, *The Chronicle-Herald*, Halifax

PETERSON, *The Vancouver Sun*

DE ADDER, *The Halifax Daily News*

PASCAL, *The Gazette*, Montreal

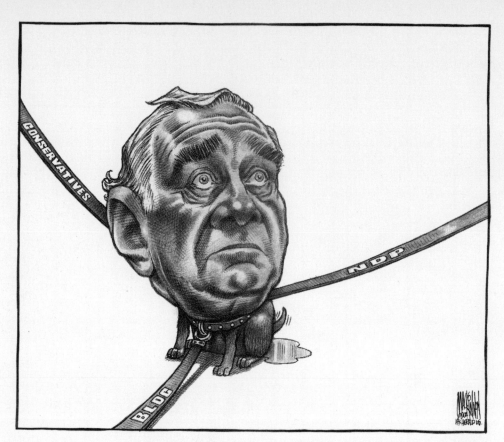

MACKINNON, *The Chronicle-Herald, Halifax*

TAB, *The Calgary Sun*

GRASTON, *The Windsor Star*

MACKAY, *The Hamilton Spectator*

BIOGRAPHIES

AISLIN is the name of TERRY MOSHER's eldest daughter and the *nom de plume* that he has used as the editorial page cartoonist for *The Gazette* in Montreal, where he has worked since 1972. Mosher is also cartoon editor of *Maclean's*, Canada's national magazine. Part of his mandate includes increasing the national profile of young, aspiring Canadian cartoonists. He has produced thirty-seven books, either collections of his own works or books that he has illustrated. Mosher also wrote, with journalist Peter Desbarats, *The Hecklers*, a history of political cartooning in Canada, published in 1980. The recipient of many awards, Terry Mosher was appointed, in May of 2003, Officer of the Order of Canada. He is a member of the board of directors for The Old Brewery Mission, Montreal's largest homeless shelter.

aislin@thegazette.canwest.com
www.aislin.com
http://cagle.slate.msn.com/politicalcartoons/

Born in 1952 in South Africa, DAVID ANDERSON (**ANDY**) was cartoonist for several newspapers in that country including *The Rand Daily Mail* until its closure in 1985 and then for *The Johannesburg Star*. He moved to Toronto with his wife and three sons in 1990, from where he continued to send back two editorial cartoons a week to *The Star* for the next 12 years. He currently freelances and his work has appeared regularly in *The National Post* and *The Globe and Mail*, among others.

david@d-andersonillustration.com
www.d-andersonillustration.com

GRAHAME ARNOULD was born in Manhattan in 1958 and some 19 years later studied economics at Queen's University in Kingston, Ontario. Upon graduation he decided to become a cartoonist. On the strength of this work, he entered the world of advertising where almost all his best work involved cartoons. His ad work won awards in Canada, the U.S., Austria and Germany. He currently lives in Vancouver where he contributes weekly editorial cartoons and illustrations to *The Georgia Straight*. His gag cartoons are also distributed through the Cartoonists and Writers Syndicate in the U.S.

g_arnould@straight.com

BADO is GUY BADEAUX's last name pro-nounced phonetically. Born in Montreal in 1949, he worked there for 10 years before moving to Ottawa in 1981 to become the editorial page cartoonist for *Le Droit*. Author of eight collec-tions of his own work and winner of the 1991 National Newspaper Award, he serves as treasurer of the Association of Canadian Editorial Cartoonists.

bado@ledroit.com
www.artizans.com
http://cagle.slate.msn.com/politicalcartoons/

PAUL BORDELEAU was born in 1967. He started out as an illustrator working for advertising agencies before having a shot at caricature; first in *VOIR-Québec* in 1992, and then also for *VOIR-Outaouais*.

paul@bordeleau.qc.ca
www.bordeleau.qc.ca
www.artizans.com

CAM (Cameron Cardow) was born and raised in Ottawa. A National Newspaper Award winner, as well as a numerous nominee, his cartoons have been published in *The New York Times*, *Los Angeles Times, USA Today, Globe and Mail, National Post, Toronto Star* and many others. He current-ly resides in Abbotsford, B.C. and draws cartoons for the *Ottawa Citizen* through the magic of the internet. His work is now syndicated through Cagle Cartoons.

cam@syndicam.com
http://caglecartoons.com
http://cagle.slate.msn.com/politicalcartoons/

GARY CLEMENT was born in Toronto in 1959. Over the past ten years his illustrations have appeared in *The New York Times*, *The Wall St. Journal*, *The Boston Globe*, *The Globe and Mail*, *The Financial Post*, *The Washington Post*, *The Medical Post* and several other *Posts*. He has also written and illustrated two children's books: *Just Stay Put* (fall 96) and *The Great Poochini* (fall 99), which won the Governor General's Award for Illustration. Winner of four National Magazine Awards as well as awards from the Advertising & Design Club of Canada, *Applied Arts* magazine, American Illustration and The American Society of Newspaper Design. He lives in Toronto with his wife, two kids and various members of the animal kingdom.

gclement@nationalpost.com
www.nationalpost.com
http://cagle.slate.msn.com/politicalcartoons/

Born in Toronto in 1951, **PATRICK CORRIGAN** studied fine arts at the Ontario College of Art, which led to a career of night-shift taxi driving. He forsook his extensive art training and freelanced for *The Financial Post*, *Maclean's* and *The Toronto Star*. He joined *The Star* in 1983 as a full-time illustrator, while filling in for Duncan Macpherson whenever possible. Three times nominated for a National Newspaper Award, he has won several awards in illustration and graphics (Society of Newspaper Design, New York Art Directors Club, Advertising Design Club of Canada, Toronto Art Directors Club). He was named the editorial page cartoonist in 1995 at *The Toronto Star* and can still quote you a return fare from the airport.

corrigan@thestar.ca
www.corrigan.ca
www.thestar.com
http://cagle.slate.msn.com/politicalcartoons/

AMERICAN GOTHIC   CANADIAN CONTEMPORARY

ANDRÉ-PHILIPPE COTÉ, born in 1955, has been the editorial cartoonist of *Le Soleil* in Quebec City since the summer of 1997. Author of the comic strip "*Baptiste*", he has also worked for the humour magazine *Safarir* in the past decade. He has published seventeen books so far and was a finalist for this year's National Newspaper Award.

apcote@lesoleil.com

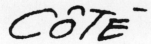

Born in 1948 in St. Thomas, Ontario, **DALE CUMMINGS** studied animation and illustration at Sheridan College in Oakville. During a brief stay in New York, he did some cartoons for *The New York Times*. He returned to Toronto in 1976, where he freelanced for *Last Post, Canadian Forum, Maclean's, The Toronto Star, Canadian Magazine* and *This Magazine*. Full-time editorial cartoonist with *The Winnipeg Free Press* since 1981, he won the National Newspaper Award in 1983.

www.artizans.com
http://cagle.slate.msn.com/politicalcartoons/

PATRICK DEA was born in Montreal in 1965. Since 1984, his work has graced the pages of countless magazines and advertising. Formally caricaturist in the humour magazine *Safarir,* and more recently with *Kamikaz*, he now does two drawings a week for Montreal's daily *La Presse* as well as replacing Bado at Ottawa's *Le Droit* during his holidays. Musician in his spare time, he practises classical guitar.

patimage@ca.inter.net
www.portfolios.com/dea
www.artizans.com

MICHAEL DeADDER was born in Moncton, New Brunswick, in 1967. Full-time cartoonist at *The Halifax Daily News* since 2000, his work has appeared in various newspapers in Canada. After graduating from Mount Allison University in 1991, with a Bachelor of Arts degree in Fine Arts, he began working as an artist out of Halifax. Realizing that he needed food and shelter to survive, he sold editorial cartoons on the side. Eventually he began selling more editorial cartoons than paintings and a cartoonist was born. De Adder considers himself to be a failed painter rather than a successful cartoonist.

deadder@hfxnews.southam.ca
www.artizans.com
http://cagle.slate.msn.com/politicalcartoons/

Born in Montreal in 1949, **SUSAN DEWAR** attended high school in Toronto, went to the University of Western Ontario in London, and graduated from Toronto Teachers' College. After working in commercial art in Toronto, she freelanced for *Canadian Forum, Teen Generation, Current* and *The Toronto Sun*. She joined The *Calgary Sun* as full-time editorial cartoonist in 1984 and won the 1987 National Business Writing Award for political cartooning. In October 1988 she became the editorial cartoonist of *The Ottawa Sun*. She is the mother of James Geoffrey.

sue.dewar@tor.sunpub.com
www.canoe.ca/OttawaSun/dewar.html
www.artizans.com

DEWAR

ANTHONY DIBERARDO was born in Hamilton, Ontario, in 1976. He graduated from the University of Guelph in the late 90's with a Fine Arts degree. It was there that he began publishing his work. He is currently a freelance cartoonist

www.diberardo.com

TIM DOLIGHAN was born in 1966 and lives with his wife, Mary, and daughters, Caili and Shanna, and son John, in Oshawa, Ontario. After receiving degrees from Laurier, York and Ottawa U (none of which had anything to do with art), he started freelancing and illustrating for community newspapers in 1992. Tim currently provides the daily editorial cartoon for Rogers hi-speed Internet. His work has received several national and Ontario community newspaper awards and is published across Canada in such publications as *The Toronto Sun, The Ottawa Citizen* and various Metroland papers.

tim@ dolighan.com
http://cagle.slate.msn.com/politicalcartoons/

DUŠAN PETRIČIĆ was born in Belgrade, Yugoslavia, in 1946. He graduated from Belgrade's Academy for Applied Arts, where he also taught illustration. Editorial cartoonist for the daily *Večernje Novosti* (Evening News) and the weekly magazine *Nin,* Petričić is the author of numerous children's books and has directed many animated films. He has won several awards: Grand Prix in Tokyo, Silver medal in Istanbul, Grand Prix in Skopje, and Golden Pen in Amsterdam. In Canada since September 1993, he has had cartoons published regularly in *The Toronto Star* and the book review section of *The New York Times.*

www.thestar.com

JOHN FEWINGS was born in Simcoe, Ontario, in 1955. He began drawing caricatures of his high school teachers to piss them off and get laughs from his friends; it worked on both counts. His first editorial cartoons appeared in *The Port Dover Maple Leaf* and *The Simcoe Reformer.* He now resides in Peterborough with Gale, Josh and their Border collie, Buddy, working as a freelance graphic designer/cartoonist. His cartoons regularly appear in *The Peterborough Examiner, The Toronto Sun* and a number of other Canadian dailies.

jfewings@sympatico.ca
www.john@fewings.ca

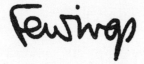

TEFLON MAN

VELCRO MAN

Christian Daigle (**FLEG**) was born in Lévis, Québec in 1963. A freelance graphic artist, illustrator and sculptor, he has been a collaborator to the daily newspaper *Le Soleil* since May 2002. His interest for caricature was sparked by his meeting with Robert LaPalme in the early 80's. Recipiant of the J.W. Bengough Award in 1979 and Albéric Bourgeois Prize in 1980, his passion is the history of caricature.

flegzo@total.net

PRÉSIDENT DE GUERRE

THOMAS SZLUKOVENYI

Born in 1949 in Saskatoon, **BRIAN GABLE** studied fine arts at the University of Saskatchewan. Graduating with a B.Ed. from the University of Toronto in 1971, he taught art in Brockville and began freelancing for the Brockville *Recorder and Times* in 1977. In 1980 he started full-time with the Regina *Leader-Post* and is presently the editorial cartoonist for *The Globe and Mail*. He has won National Newspaper Awards in 1986, 1995 and 2001.

bgable@globeandmail.ca
www.globeandmail.ca
http://cagle.slate.msn.com/politicalcartoons/

FRANÇOIS DESAULNIERS

Born in Montreal in 1951, and after studies having nothing to do with drawing, MICHEL GARNEAU (**GARNOTTE**) has contributed to many newspapers and magazines in Montreal, including *CROC, TV Hebdo, Protégez-vous (Protect Yourself), Titanic* (of which he was editor-in-chief), *Les Expos, Je me petit-débrouille, La Terre de chez nous* and *Nouvelles CSN*. He became the editorial cartoonist for *Le Devoir* in April 1996.

garnotte@ledevoir.ca
www.ledevoir.com

GARNOTTE

Born in Montreal in 1964, **ÉRIC GODIN** is an illustrator, graphic artist and painter. He was the first daily online cartoonist in Quebec, did a daily cartoon at television network TVA and worked, for 11 years, at *Voir*, a Montreal weekly. He is currently the art director at *La Tribune* in Sherbrooke, Quebec and draws a weekly cartoon in the business section at Montreal's *La Presse*.

studio@ericgodin.com

MIKE GRASTON was born and raised in Montreal. He has been editorial cartoonist with the *Windsor Star* since 1980, after having spent time obtaining an honours degree in history from the University of Western Ontario and freelancing for *The Ottawa Citizen*. His work has appeared in most Canadian newspapers as well as a number of American publications and has been featured on ABC's *Nightline*, CBC, CTV and *CBC Newsworld*. He has three daughters: Lisa, Carly and Raquel.

grastoon@cogeco.ca
mgraston@thestar.canwest.com
www.grastoon.com
http://cagle.slate.msn.com/politicalcartoons/

Born in Liverpool, **GRAHAM HARROP** emigrated to Canada at the constant urging of friends, family and the British Government. He has worked in a mill, as a paint store clerk and once drove cab in a gorilla suit. He draws the gag panel *Back Bench* for *The Globe and Mail*, editorial cartoons for *The Vancouver Sun* and, on Wednesdays, a fake moustache on his upper lip.

www.artizans.com
www.cagle.com

ANTHONY JENKINS was born and raised in Toronto and spent his early career delivering *The Globe and Mail*. A U of T/University of Waterloo BA grad, he joined the paper in 1974 after a summer at the *Toronto Star*. In the 1980s he took three year-long leaves of absence to travel in 74 countries. During the 1980s, he also began writing for the paper and has fine art pretensions as a portrait painter. The bastard is not bad at it and is getting better. He draws caricatures at *The Globe* and lives in Toronto with spouse and two oft-painted daughters.

ajenkins@globeandmail.ca
www.jenkinsdraws.com

BOB KRIEGER has actually managed to hold a job drawing editorial cartoons for *The Province* newspaper since 1981. Go figure. When he's not working, the Vancouver native likes to cook, eat, drink, play a little guitar and start rumours regarding the impending political comeback of Bill Vander Zalm... essentially anything to get out of doing yard work.

bkrieger@telus.net
www.artizans.com

PATRICK LAMONTAGNE was born in Red Deer, Alberta in 1971. Having been the editorial cartoonist for the *Banff Crag & Canyon* for three years, he relocated to *The Rocky Mountain Outlook* in September of 2001. Cartoon Ink syndicated a national editorial cartoon in October of 2001. Patrick's cartoons regularly appear in a number of weekly and daily newspapers across Canada, including *The Calgary Herald, The Montreal Gazette, The Vancouver Sun,* and *The Ottawa Citizen.* He is a regular contributing cartoonist to *Maclean's.* Patrick is also a freelance writer and illustrator. He and his wife, Shonna, live in Canmore, Alberta in the midst of the Canadian Rockies.

cartoon@cartoonink.com
www.cartoonink.com

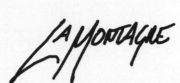

JACK LEFCOURT was born in 1964 in Kitchener, Ontario. He studied Fine Arts and History at the University of Waterloo where he also began his cartooning career, drawing campus-related panels for the student newspaper. His work has appeared in dailies, entertainment and community weeklies, and various magazines across Canada and elsewhere since he began drawing professionally in 1989. In the past four years, Lefcourt has developed an online web gallery of his work and has produced seven bound collections available through his site.

jack@lefcourtland.com
www.lefcourtland.com

GARETH LIND, 40, has been cartooning for almost as long as he can remember. His satirical comic strip, *Weltschmerz*, has appeared in Toronto's *eye* weekly and other Ontario alternative papers since 1996. An additional political cartoon appears nationally in *This Magazine*. Lind is based in Guelph, Ontario, where he is a full-time, self-employed graphic designer. In between his drafting table and his computer, he catches a little life.

lind@lindtoons.com
www.weltschmerz.ca

LIND

Born in Hamilton in 1968, **GRAEME MACKAY**, is *The Hamilton Spectator's* resident editorial cartoonist. This self-proclaimed "news geek" grew up in Dundas. Except for a few (long ago) Saturday morning art classes at the Dundas Valley School of Art, Graeme's skill in cartooning is largely self-taught. After studying politics and history at the University of Ottawa, he travelled Europe with pen and sketchbook in hand. In 1997, he began his professional career at *The Hamilton Spectator*. MacKay's cartoons have appeared in newspapers across Canada and the US in addition to various magazines and periodicals including *Macleans*. Graeme and his wife, Wendi, live in Hamilton with their daughter, Gillian.

gmackay@hamiltonspectator.com
www.mackaycartoons.net
http://cagle.slate.msn.com/politicalcartoons/

MACKAY

BRUCE MACKINNON grew up in Antigonish, Nova Scotia, studied fine arts at Mount Allison University, and was a member of the Graphic Design program at the Nova Scotia College of Art and Design. He started doing a weekly editorial cartoon with *The Halifax Herald* in 1985, working at home while raising his newborn daughter, Robyn. Through the miracle of day-care, he was able to join *The Herald* on a full-time basis in August of 1986. He has won several Atlantic Journalism Awards for editorial cartooning, was named "journalist of the year" in 1991, and was the National Newspaper Award winner for both 1992 and 1993.

mackinnonb@herald.ca
www.herald.ns.ca
http://cagle.slate.msn.com/politicalcartoons/
www.artizans.com

MALCOLM MAYES was born in Edmonton in 1962. Editorial cartoonist for *The Edmonton Journal* since June 1986, his work has appeared in most major Canadian newspapers and many major American newspapers, as well as numerous books and magazines including *Best Editorial Cartoons of the Year* (USA), *Reader's Digest*, and *The Great Big Book of Canadian Humour*. In addition, his cartoons have been featured on CBC, CNN, and at Montreal's International Museum of Humour.

mmayes@artizans.com
www.artizans.com

J.J. McCULLOUGH was born in Vancouver, British Columbia in 1984 and is currently a student at BC's Simon Fraser University. He has drawn for a variety of different Vancouver publications on a freelance basis, and is currently the staff cartoonist at the Douglas College Student newspaper, the *Other Press*. Though he is yet to be published in any serious publication, his thrice-weekly editorial cartoons receive a lot of exposure on his popular website.

wart_mamu@yahoo.co
www.filibustercartoons.com

THEO MOUDAKIS (**MOU**) was born in Montreal in 1965 where he began freelancing for *The Gazette* in 1986. In 1991 he started full-time with *The Halifax Daily News* and in September 2000 became editorial cartoonist for *The Toronto Star*. His work has appeared in most Canadian dailies as well as *The New York Times*, *Time* and *Mad*, and has been three times short-listed for the National Newspaper Award.

mou@thestar.ca
www.thestar.com

154.

DAN MURPHY was born in Missouri. He moved to Canada in the early seventies, drawing for various underground newspapers and aboveground magazines. He is a cartoonist and columnist for the Vancouver *Province*.

dmurphy@png.canwest.com
www.artizans.com

Born in 1955 in Woodbridge, Ontario, **STEVE NEASE** is art director of *The Oakville Beaver*, producing regular editorial cartoons and his family humour comic strip, *Pud*, which are both syndicated by Miller Features. Nease is a four-time recipient of the Canadian Community Newspapers Awards for cartooning. He and his wife Dian live in Oakville, and have four sons: Robert, Ben, Sam and Max.

snease@haltonsearch.com
http://cagle.slate.msn.com/politicalcartoons/

Born in 1969, NIKAHANG KOWSAR (**NIK**) studied geology at Tehran University. He has worked for more than 20 Iranian newspapers (mostly banned by the Press court) in the past 13 years. His work is published worlwide through Cartoonists and Writers Syndicate. Nik was imprisoned for drawing a cartoon in February 2000 and faced prosecution in Iran for more than 160 of his published cartoons before his arrest. His life has been threatened several times, the latest in October 2003 and he fears going back to Iran. Member of the board of directors of Cartoonists Rights Network International, he has been a three times winner of the Crystal Pen, given to Iran's best journalists. His international awards include the 2001 International Award of Courage in Editorial Cartooning, and the second prize in the National Press Club of Canada's editorial cartoon contest in 2001. He has published 6 books, 4 of them best sellers in Iran.

Prairie-born **GEOFF OLSON** has worked for *The Vancouver Courier* for, like, ages. His artwork and articles have also appeared in *Maclean's* magazine, *The Vancouver Sun, The Globe and Mail, Common Ground* magazine, and many other publications.

gefo@telus.net
www.geocities.com/SoHo/Gallery/3452/

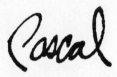

PASCAL ÉLIE was born in Montreal in 1959. His cartoons are published twice a week (on Sundays and Mondays) in the Montreal *Gazette*. He's also the regular cartoonist for the business weekly *Les Affaires* and contributes to *Law Times*, as well as for several other publications in Quebec and English Canada. He's been freelancing for a couple of decades, but left his day-job (as a legal editor) to become a full-time cartoonist in January 1998.

pascalelie@videotron.ca

GREG PERRY fell to earth in British Columbia during the '60s and learned to draw by studying prehistoric cave art. His history in newspaper is long and boring with many years spent at a variety of journals with no circulation. He was sued by the CEO of a public utility, made headlines for making Premier Bernard Lord cry and has been unanimously condemned by the New Brunswick legislature and various municipal councils. Now syndicated, Perry's cartoons appear daily across Canada.

perryink@rogers.com
http://cagle.slate.msn.com/politicalcartoons/

Winnipeg-born, **ROY PETERSON** works for *The Vancouver Sun*. His work has appeared in all major Canadian and many American newspapers and magazines. He has produced many covers, illustrations and cartoons for *Maclean's*, including his 23-year association with Allan Fotheringham's Back Page column. His books include *The World According to Roy Peterson*, *Drawn & Quartered*, *The Canadian ABC Book* and the best-selling *Frog Fables and Beaver Tales* series with Stanley Burke. Recently widowed, Roy and Margaret raised five children. He has served as president of both the Canadian and American Associations of Editorial Cartoonists. Winner of the Grand Prize at the Salon of Caricature in Montreal and seven National Newspaper Awards, he was appointed this year Officer of the Order of Canada.

petersoninkinc@shaw.ca
www.artizans.com
http://cagle.slate.msn.com/politicalcartoons/

JIM PHILLIPS was born in 1956, along with twin brother John, in Newmarket and raised in Jackson's Point, Ontario. Beginning his career in editorial cartooning at the age of 15 at *The Lake Simcoe Advocate*, he attended illustration and cartooning classes at Sheridan College and for a brief time studied at the Ontario College of Art. Winner of five Ontario and Canadian community newspaper awards for cartooning, he was the author of the daily cartoon (*SUNtoon*) published in *The Toronto Sun* from 1980 until this year and syndicated his editorial cartoons through his website. He drew a few animated cartoons during the last election campaign for *The Globe and Mail's* and CTV's websites.

www.nationalheckle.com
http://cagle.slate.msn.com/politicalcartoons/

INGRID RICE is a self-syndicated cartoonist published in over 50 markets across Canada and throughout British Columbia. Although she has not won any contests, she has appeared before the B.C. Press Council and been found to be reprehensible. Her free time is spent caring for assorted guinea pigs and a cat.

ouridea@shaw.ca

Born in Edmonton in 1946, **VANCE RODEWALT** did advertising cartoons at *The Roughneck* after completing high school. Working for Marvel Comics for five years, he travelled to Europe and, upon his return, began doing political cartoons for the Calgary *Albertan*. When the *Albertan* was bought by *The Calgary Sun,* he remained there for 3 1/2 years before moving on to *The Calgary Herald* where he shared editorial page cartooning duties with Tom Innes. He has assumed full duties since 1987 and won the 1988 National Newspaper Award for Cartooning. Vance also drew the internationally syndicated *Chubb & Chauncey* comic strip. He and his wife, a former champion figure skater, live in Calgary and have two sons.

vrodewalt@theherald.canwest.com
http://cagle.slate.msn.com/politicalcartoons/

DAVE ROSEN was born in Montreal in 1955 and started drawing for the alternative press at the age of 16. Over the years, he has contributed to *The Canadian Encyclopedia*, worked as a stand-up comic and been arrested for inciting a riot. He is currently a traffic reporter for CBC Radio and his cartoons appear in the *Montreal Mirror*.
He has also published three books, none of which will be made into a movie.

toons@ca.inter.net
www.artizans.com

FRED SEBASTIAN was born (in 1964) and bred in Ottawa. A graduate of Algonquin College's Commercial Art/Graphic Design program, his work appears in *Legion* and *The New York Times Book Review*. In 1994, he won a *Studio* magazine merit award for illustration and, in 2001, the National Press Club International Editorial Cartoon Competition On Press Freedom.

sebastian@magma.ca
www.artizans.com
www.reuben.org/sebastian

SHAHID MAHMOOD, born in 1971, grew up in Pakistan during General Zia's military rule. He started drawing for *The Star*, Karachi's evening newspaper, at the age of 15. He went on to become the editorial cartoonist for both the national newspaper in Pakistan, *Dawn*, and news-magazine, *Newsline*. A style described by editors as "irreverent and dark," his work has appeared in numerous Pakistani, North American and international publications and manages to continuously enrage Benazir Bhutto.

shahid@drawnconclusions.com

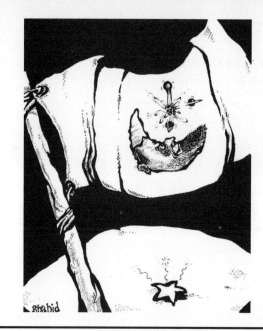

THOMAS BOLDT (**TAB**) was born in Southern Prussia to a family of shepherds. Having survived the Industrial Revolution, he came to Canada only to find the market for shepherds on the verge of collapse. Tab draws cartoons for *The Calgary Sun*.

www.canoe.ca/CalgarySun/boldt.html
http://cagle.slate.msn.com/politicalcartoons/

MICHAEL ZAHARUK was born in Toronto in 1965. Graduating from the Ontario College of Art in 1991, he has been working as an illustrator and freelance editorial cartoonist ever since. His illustration work has been featured in *Time* magazine, *The Wall Street Journal*, *The Chicago Tribune*, *New York* magazine and *The Toronto Star*. His editorial cartoons are syndicated by Artizans.

zaharuk@sympatico.ca
www.artizans.com

IN ADDITION TO PORTFOOLIO, HERE IS A LIST OF OUR CONTRIBUTORS RECENT COLLECTIONS

AISLIN, *Oh! Oh! A Collection of the Best of Aislin From the Last Three Years*. Introduction by Dick Pound, McArthur & Company, 2004

GORDON SNELL, *Further Fabulous Canadians! More Hysterically Historical Rhymes* with illustrations by Aislin, McArthur & Company, 2004

BADO, *Bado 2004 et même plus !*, Les éditions L'Interligne, Ottawa, 2004

CHAPLEAU, *L'année Chapleau,* Boréal, 2004

CÔTÉ, *De tout les Côté 2004,* Éditions Le Soleil, 2004

GARNOTTE, *Les plus meilleures caricatures de Garnotte en 2003,* Éditions du Concassé, 2003